A Kid's Kosher COOKING CRUISE

Mildred L. Covert
and Sylvia P. Gerson

Illustrated by Alan Gerson

A FIREBIRD PRESS BOOK

Gretna 2008

Copyright © 1997
By Mildred L. Covert and Sylvia P. Gerson
All rights reserved

First printing, September 1997
Second printing, July 2008

The word "Pelican" and the depiction of a pelican are trademarks of Pelican Publishing Company, Inc., and are registered in the U.S. Patent and Trademark Office.

Library of Congress Cataloging-in-Publication Data

Covert, Mildred L.
    A kid's kosher cooking cruise / by Mildred L. Covert and Sylvia P. Gerson ; illustrated by Alan Gerson.
      p. cm.
    Includes index.
    Summary: Includes Jewish and southern recipes from cities which Hannah and Hershel visit while on a cruise up the Mississippi River; also provides history and geography of places visited.
    ISBN 978-1-56554-225-9 (pbk. : alk. paper)
    1. Cookery, Jewish—Juvenile literature. 2. Cookery, American—Southern style—Juvenile literature. [1. Cookery, Jewish. 2. Cookery, American—Southern style.] I. Gerson, Sylvia P. II. Gerson, Alan, ill. III. Title.
TX724.C6797 1997   96-54605
641.5'376—dc21   CIP
                                                                                                                  AC

Firebird, Firebird Press, and 🕊 are imprints of Firebird Press, Inc.
a division of Pelican Publishing Company, Inc.

Printed in the United States of America
Published by Pelican Publishing Company, Inc.
1000 Burmaster Street, Gretna, Louisiana 70053

A Kid's Kosher
COOKING CRUISE

*Dedicated to the grandparents who inspired us and
the grandchildren we hope to inspire*

Contents

Introduction: Welcome Aboard 9
              Signs and Symbols
              Did You Know?
              Abbreviations
              Standard Metric Approximations
Hannah and Hershel at School 15
New Orleans 17
Baton Rouge 23
Natchez 29
Vicksburg 33
Little Rock 39
Memphis 45
Hannibal 51
Shalom 57
Index 59

Introduction: Welcome Aboard

Join the twins, Hershel and Hannah, and their grandmother as they board the *Simcha Ship* for a cruise up the Mississippi River. Come along and visit each port with them. Learn from Chef Lazér how to cook the recipes the children liked best from each city they visited.

We wrote them all down for you in this book so you, too, could share not only in the twins' cooking classes, but also in their adventures while learning history and geography—all in an easy and fun-filled way.

So here's to happy sailing and happy cooking!

MILDRED L. COVERT
and
SYLVIA P. GERSON

SIGNS AND SYMBOLS

1 Star of David = easiest;
   no help needed. You can do it alone.
2 Stars of David = easier;
   takes a little more work, but you can do it.
3 Stars of David = easy.
   You can still do it, but with adult assistance.
Star of David with (*D*) = dairy food
Star of David with (*M*) = meat products
Star of David with (*P*) = pareve (food that can be eaten with either dairy or meat)
Star of David with (*D/P*) = can be made dairy or pareve

DID YOU KNOW?

3 teaspoons = 1 tablespoon
4 tablespoons = ¼ cup
8 tablespoons = ½ cup
1 cup = 8 ounces
2 cups = 1 pint
2 pints = 1 quart
1 pound butter or margarine = 4 sticks
1 cup butter or margarine = 2 sticks
1 pound sifted flour = 4 cups
1 pound granulated sugar = 2 to 2¼ cups
1 pound confectioners (powdered) sugar = 4 to 4½ cups
2 large eggs = 3 small eggs

ABBREVIATIONS

STANDARD

tsp.	=	teaspoon
tbsp.	=	tablespoon
oz.	=	ounce
qt.	=	quart
lb.	=	pound

METRIC

ml.	=	milliliter
l.	=	liter
g.	=	gram
kg.	=	kilogram
mg.	=	milligram

STANDARD METRIC APPROXIMATIONS

LIQUID MEASUREMENTS

⅛ teaspoon	=	.6 milliliter
¼ teaspoon	=	1.2 milliliters
½ teaspoon	=	2.5 milliliters
1 teaspoon	=	5 milliliters
1 tablespoon	=	15 milliliters
4 tablespoons	=	¼ cup = 60 milliliters
8 tablespoons	=	½ cup = 118 milliliters
16 tablespoons	=	1 cup = 236 milliliters
2 cups	=	473 milliliters
2½ cups	=	563 milliliters
4 cups	=	946 milliliters
1 quart	=	4 cups = .94 liter

SOLID MEASUREMENTS

½ ounce	=	15 grams
1 ounce	=	25 grams
4 ounces	=	110 grams
16 ounces	=	1 pound = 454 grams

A Kid's Kosher
COOKING CRUISE

HANNAH AND HERSHEL AT SCHOOL

As Hannah and Hershel, the twins, were preparing for the first day of school, their mother reminded them to be sure to bring some of the interesting pictures they took on their vacation.

Hershel and Hannah not only packed their pictures, but also some of their favorite souvenirs.

The school bus honked its horn loud and clear. The twins grabbed their lunch and their backpacks and ran excitedly to the bus.

As the bus pulled into the school yard, the principal was waiting to greet all the boys and girls and show them to their classrooms. While walking down the hall the children were waving and calling out to each other. As the twins turned toward their classroom, there was Ms. Farrell, their new teacher, standing in the doorway, smiling and greeting each student and assigning them their seats as they entered.

Soon the class was filled and when Ms. Farrell stood in front of the class, tapping her ruler on the desk, all the noise and commotion stopped.

"Welcome to my class. I'm very glad to meet you all," she said. "I know every one of you had a wonderful summer. Before I hand out the books, I would like to hear how each of you spent your vacation. Suppose Hannah and Hershel start."

Hershel was so excited that before he even got to the front of the class he blurted out, "My grandmother lives in New Orleans, right on the Mississippi River, and every summer we go to see her."

By now, Hannah was in front of the class at Hershel's side. She said, "This summer, what a surprise she had for us! She took us on a steamboat trip up the Mississippi River. The boat, which was called the *Simcha Ship*, had a big red paddlewheel that turned and turned in the water."

Hershel interrupted. "And the captain told us that long ago

thousands of Indians like the Choctaws and Cherokees rode on a boat to get to their reservations. Then he showed us the calliope that was on our boat. Hannah loved that. Go ahead, you can tell the class about it."

"You know, it's really a musical instrument," Hannah added, "that has a whole lot of steam whistles on it and each whistle plays a different note. It sounds like a church organ. Anyway, that's where the music comes from. And when you hear it you just feel like dancing all around the ship."

"That's not all," chimed in Hershel. "I went up one day to where they steer the boat and the river pilot let me hold the wheel for a while."

Ms. Farrell turned to the twins. "That must have been an exciting trip for you both. You must have learned a lot of history and geography on board and in the different ports you visited."

She continued, "Hannah, tell us about some of those cities. What did you see and do? I'm sure the class would like to hear about that."

NEW ORLEANS

"Hershel and I have been to New Orleans plenty of times," said Hannah. "And we always love to walk through the French Quarter. Grandmother told us the people down there sometimes call it by the French name, the Vieux Carré. It's fun to see all the free entertainers like the mimes and the tap dancers, and we always get hot chocolate and beignets—that's French, too, for the doughnuts they make down there. They sprinkle them with powdered sugar while they are still hot and boy, are they good! And we both love the hot, buttered corn on the cob the street vendors sell. They put a stick into the cob and you can walk around and eat it just like you would an ice cream cone or popsicle, only the butter melts instead of the ice cream."

"When you walk around the French Quarter," Hershel interrupted, "you can hear and see all the jazz musicians just playing away and artists busy painting pictures—all right out there on the streets and sidewalks."

"This summer," Hershel continued, "Grandmother had something new to show us. It was the Aquarium of the Americas, which was right on the riverfront where our ship was docked. Hannah didn't think she would like the Aquarium because she's afraid of sharks and alligators. But we soon found out that all the fish, penguins, and reptiles were behind glass."

Ms. Farrell asked, "Was there some special activity on your cruise that the two of you shared that was different or unusual?"

"Oh, yes," answered Hannah. "We went to a children's cooking class. At first I didn't think Hershel would like that, until he found out that a lot of famous cooks are men."

Hershel admitted that he had had a lot of fun. "Even the ship's cook was a man. He was the one who taught the class. We learned how to make a lot of good things. Every morning, before we would dock, Chef Lazér—that was the chef's name, he is a famous Kosher chef—would have the cooking class and tell us about the city and what the people in that city like to eat. That's what we would learn to cook that day."

"Chef Lazér told us that New Orleans is famous for food," Hannah chimed in. "He handed us aprons and we were all excited as we put them on. When we saw Chef Lazér put on his high white *toque*—that's what he called his chef's cap—we knew we were ready to cook New Orleans food."

PADDLEWHEEL FISH BALLS ✡ ✡ ✡ (P)

You will need:

peanut oil (enough to measure 1 inch deep in frying pan)
1 16-oz. jar small gefilte fish balls
½ cup matzo meal
1 measuring cup
1 frying pan
1 colander
2 flat platters
paper towels
1 slotted spoon
pot holders

How to:

1. Pour peanut oil into a frying pan and heat oil until hot.
2. While oil is heating, drain fish in colander.
3. Pour matzo meal onto a flat platter.
4. Place paper towels on the other platter and set aside.
5. Roll fish balls in the matzo meal. Make sure balls are well coated.
6. Drop the coated fish balls into the hot oil and fry until they are golden brown.
7. Remove the balls with slotted spoon and drain on paper towels. Remove paper towels before serving.

Serves 4.

CORNSICLES ✡ ✡ (D)

You will need:

4 ears of fresh corn
4 pats of butter
salt to taste

1 large pot
1 colander
4 wooden skewers
1 pastry brush
pot holders

How to:

1. Remove the husks and silk from the ears of corn.
2. Place the corn in a large pot and add enough cold water to cover it.
3. Cover the pot and heat over high heat to boiling; then boil 2 to 3 minutes.
4. Drain the corn in a colander.
5. Push a wooden skewer into the top of each corn cob. Brush with a pat of butter and sprinkle with salt.

Serves 4.

BEN-YEAHS ✡ ✡ ✡ (D/P)

You will need:

oil for deep frying
½ cup sugar
1 tsp. cinnamon
1½ cups Kosher biscuit mix
½ cup milk or water
1 cup powdered sugar

measuring cups
measuring spoons
1 deep frying pan
2 platters
paper towels
1 mixing bowl
1 stirring spoon
plastic wrap
1 rolling pin
biscuit cutter
1 knife
1 slotted spoon
1 brown paper bag
pot holders

How to:

1. Pour at least 2 inches of oil into deep frying pan.
2. Line 1 platter with paper towels and set aside.
3. Mix sugar and cinnamon together and pour onto second platter. Set aside.
4. In bowl, mix together the biscuit mix and milk or water.
5. Sprinkle some additional biscuit mix on a counter top.
6. Put dough on floured counter and knead 3 or 4 times.
7. Place plastic wrap over dough. With rolling pin, roll dough until it is about ½-inch thick.
8. Remove plastic wrap and cut dough with biscuit cutter. Then cut each biscuit in half.
9. Dip each biscuit half in the sugar and cinnamon mix. Turn biscuit over and dip other side in sugar and cinnamon mix.
10. Heat the oil until very hot, but not smoking.
11. Place a biscuit on the slotted spoon and carefully lower biscuit into hot oil.
12. The biscuits will brown quickly, so watch them, and turn them over once as they brown.
13. As soon as it is brown on the other side, remove doughnut with slotted spoon and drain it on the paper towels.
14. Put the cup of powdered sugar in the brown bag. Drop the warm, drained doughnuts into the bag, fold down the top of the bag, and shake the bag several times until all the doughnuts are covered with the sugar.
15. Remove doughnuts from the bag and serve while still warm.

Makes 16 doughnuts.

QUARTER QUENCHER ✡ (P)

You will need:

1 cup lemon juice
1 cup lime juice
¾ cup sugar
1 qt. orange juice
16-oz. bottle club soda
ice
lime slices

measuring cups
punch bowl
1 stirring spoon

How to:

1. In a punch bowl, mix lemon juice, lime juice, and sugar together, stirring until sugar dissolves.
2. Put the bowl in the refrigerator until it gets cold.
3. When you are ready to serve, add the club soda and ice, and stir well.
4. Place a lime slice on the rim of each glass.

Makes 1½ gallons (about 12 glasses).

BATON ROUGE

The morning after they got on the boat and enjoyed their first cooking class, Hannah and Hershel were eating breakfast when they heard the Captain's voice on the loudspeaker. He was saying that the ship was pulling into the port of Baton Rouge, the capital city of Louisiana.

The twins ran to the deck and watched as the ship was tied to the dock. They saw the tour buses waiting to take them on a sightseeing tour. With an OK from Grandmother, Hershel and Hannah ran toward the bus and jumped on. They wanted a front seat where they could see everything.

The tour guide said, "Our first stop will be the Louisiana State Capitol, the nation's tallest capitol building."

Hershel and Hannah learned that there are 50 stairs leading up to the entrance of the capitol, each step standing for one of the 50 states.

Inside the capitol, the twins took the elevator to the 27th floor to get to the observation deck. They had fun seeing all of Baton Rouge and the river from so high up. The ships looked like little toy boats, and they tried to see which one was their *Simcha Ship*.

After lunch Hannah and Hershel were the first ones back on the bus, eagerly waiting for the tour guide to tell them what was coming next.

The tour guide picked up his microphone. "We are going on a swamp tour. Here you will see what lives and grows in Louisiana's bayous and marshes."

The group got on the swamp boat. Someone asked the Cajun guide if they would see any alligators or crocodiles. "Sure, plenty!" he answered. "But you'll only see alligators here in Louisiana. Many people get alligators and crocodiles mixed up, but you can tell the difference by looking at the snout. The alligator's snout is rounded, while the crocodile's comes to a point. Crocodiles live in Florida and tropical waters."

Sure enough, soon the group saw alligators swimming toward them. It was scary. But the guide told everyone not to be afraid. Then he said that he was going to hand feed them from the covered boat.

"Boy! Is he ever brave!" gasped Hannah.

After the alligators left, she was the first one to see the birds. The guide said that they were blue herons and egrets. They were beautiful. Then the twins saw a white-tailed deer running into the bushes.

Grandmother loved the plants and flowers and big cypress trees with hanging moss.

It was an exciting day and even the twins were glad to get back on board the ship and call it a day.

Bright and early the next morning, Chef Lazér and his students began their first lesson in Cajun cooking, the Kosher way!

CAPITOL CHICKEN ✡ ✡ ✡ (M)

You will need:

6 boneless chicken breasts
2 eggs
1 cup water
1 cup flour
1 tsp. salt
¼ tsp. black pepper
vegetable oil for frying

measuring cups
measuring spoons
1 sharp knife
1 cutting board
1 mixing bowl
1 large mixing spoon
1 deep frying pan
1 slotted spoon
1 flat platter covered with paper towels
pot holders

How to:

1. Cut the chicken breasts into 1-inch by 1½-inch pieces.
2. In a bowl, mix eggs and water together.
3. Add flour, salt, and pepper to make the batter.
4. Fill frying pan ⅓ full with oil. Heat oil until hot.
5. Dip chicken pieces into batter. Drain off excess batter.
6. Carefull lower coated chicken pieces into hot oil. Fry 3 to 5 minutes, or until golden brown and well done.
7. Drain on paper towels.

Serves 6.

SPAGHETTI WITH SWAMP SAUCE ✡ ✡ (P)

You will need:

1 8-oz. package spaghetti
1 28-oz. can tomato puree
1 8-oz. can tomato sauce
1 tsp. dried oregano
1 tsp. dried basil

measuring spoons
1 large 3-qt. pot to cook spaghetti
1 2-qt. pot
1 can opener
1 large wooden spoon
1 colander
pot holders

How to:

1. Cook spaghetti following the directions on the package.
2. Meanwhile, in the 2-qt. pot, mix together the tomato puree, tomato sauce, oregano, and basil.
3. Cook the tomato mixture, stirring occasionally with the wooden spoon, until well heated.
4. Drain the spaghetti well in the colander.
5. Pour the sauce over the spaghetti and serve.

Serves 4.

NUTTY FRUIT SALAD ✡ (P)

You will need:

½ cup mayonnaise
1 tbsp. peanut butter
2 apples
2 bananas
lettuce leaves
¼ cup unsalted peanuts

measuring cups
measuring spoons
1 mixing bowl
1 rubber scraper
1 cutting board
1 apple corer
1 paring knife
1 large serving spoon

How to:

1. Mix mayonnaise and peanut butter in mixing bowl.
2. Use rubber scraper to stir until well mixed.
3. Wash and core the apples. Throw cores away.
4. On the cutting board, cut apples into bite-size pieces.
5. Add apple pieces to the peanut butter mixture and stir with scraper until apple pieces are coated.
6. Peel the bananas. Put them on the cutting board and slice them ½-inch thick.
7. Add banana slices to peanut butter and apple mixture.
8. Stir until all banana slices are coated.
9. Put lettuce leaves on the salad plates and spoon the apple-banana mixture onto the lettuce.
10. Sprinkle with peanuts and serve.

Serves 6.

NATCHEZ

On the second day out, the twins found themselves in another state—Mississippi. The ship was headed for Natchez, a very busy river port and a city famous for the part it played in American Southern history.

"I feel like a real Southern belle," exclaimed Hannah as she rode with Grandmother and Hershel in the open horse-drawn carriage. They were listening to the carriage driver, who was pointing out the big plantations where cotton was grown in the Old South.

The twins stopped and visited the homes on the plantations. While they walked through them, they were told all about the important part Natchez played in the Civil War. After that they got back on the carriage and the driver took them to the next stop, which was the Grand Village of the Natchez Indians.

There, they learned how the Natchez Indians hunted and built their teepees. They lived in the village until 1730, long before the Civil War. Boy! The twins were so excited listening to the Indian stories. They wanted to hear more but they were getting hungry. The driver said it was time to return to the carriage and go on to the Natchez State Park where they would fix their own lunch.

Chef Lazér, who was also on the tour, had brought all kinds of things to make a box lunch. He had bread, tuna fish, cooked potatoes, and eggs. The kids couldn't wait to put it all together like he taught them.

It was such a beautiful summer day—just the kind of day for a picnic. They all ate under a shady tree with lots of hanging moss. After lunch the park guide took the twins on a hike through the old Natchez Trail, which was first used by the Indians. Grandmother followed in the carriage with the driver and met them at the end of the trail.

Tired from the long hike, they were happy to return to the *Simcha Ship*.

PLANTATION POTATO SALAD ✡ (P)

Note: This recipe requires some preparation.

You will need:

2 large potatoes, cooked and diced
4 hard-boiled eggs, diced
2 ribs celery, cut into coarse pieces
¼ cup mayonnaise
1 tbsp. tarragon vinegar
½ tsp. onion powder
½ tsp. parsley flakes
1 tbsp. sweet pickle relish
salt and pepper to taste

1 measuring cup
measuring spoons
1 large mixing bowl
1 mixing spoon
1 small mixing bowl

How to:

1. In large mixing bowl, toss together the diced potatoes, eggs, and celery.
2. In small bowl, mix mayonnaise with the vinegar, onion powder, parsley flakes, pickle relish, salt, and pepper.
3. Pour mayonnaise mixture over potatoes, eggs, and celery. Mix well.

Serves 4.

HERSHEL'S "HERO" SANDWICH ✡ (P)

You will need:

1 6 ½-oz. can tuna fish, drained
1 tbsp. mayonnaise
1 rib celery
2 French bread rolls
ketchup, if you like

measuring spoons
1 can opener
1 mixing bowl
1 sharp knife
1 cutting board
1 mixing spoon

How to:

1. Put tuna fish and mayonnaise in the bowl.
2. Cut the celery into small pieces and mix with tuna.
3. Cut the rolls in half, lengthwise, and scoop out the middle.
4. Fill the rolls with the tuna fish mix.
5. Top with ketchup, if you like.

Serves 2.

NATCHEZ NOSH ✡ (P)

You will need:

1 cup dried apples
1 cup dried pears
1 cup dried pineapple
1 cup seedless raisins
1 cup pecan pieces
1 cup chocolate chips

measuring cups
1 large bowl
1 mixing spoon

How to:

1. Put all ingredients in the bowl.
2. Mix together and begin to nosh!

Serves 10 to 12.

VICKSBURG

Ms. Farrell knew that the *Simcha Ship* had made another stop in Mississippi—at Vicksburg. She also could tell that the twins had much more to say to the class. Since it was the "Show and Tell" period, she decided this was a good time for Hannah and Hershel to show their souvenirs. "Hershel, I see you can't wait to open your box," she said.

Hershel leaned over and pulled out his toy gunboats that looked like the ones used during the Battle of Vicksburg in 1863. Then he took out some toy soldiers, some painted blue and some painted gray, and placed them around the boats. He told the class the story that was told to him.

"You know," Hershel began, "Vicksburg was one of the South's main ports. It's between two rivers, the Mississippi and the Yazoo, and the North wanted to capture it. But Vicksburg is on what the guide called a bluff, the top of a hill. And when General Grant tried to take the city, he couldn't because the Confederate soldiers were up high and were shooting down at them. Of course, finally General Grant did win and battleships like this one were captured and the city fell to the Union soldiers."

While Hershel was talking, Hannah was getting her souvenirs ready for her turn. When he finished, Hannah was standing there holding her box. She took out her doll.

"Grandmother bought me this at the museum's gift shop."

Hannah held up the doll and let the class see that it was dressed exactly like the plantation ladies. The class giggled as Hannah picked up the doll's long dress to show the ruffled pantaloons underneath.

"I have to tell you about a show Grandmother took us to see," continued Hannah. "It was all about Vicksburg before and after the war. Of course Hershel loved all the battle scenes, but I liked the plantation scenes with the ladies in their beautiful dresses, waving at the soldiers going off to war. And on the way out, Grandmother bought a cookbook that had Vicksburg recipes, some of which she thought Chef Lazér could use in our next cooking class."

Just then, the bell rang, signaling the end of "Show and Tell."

PEANUTTY TOAST ✩ ✩ ✩ (D)

You will need:

12 slices white bread
¾ cup peanut butter
6 tbsp. jelly
3 eggs
¾ cup milk
¼ tsp. cinnamon
¼ tsp. salt
2 tbsp. butter or margarine

measuring cups
measuring spoons
1 spreading knife
1 medium mixing bowl
1 large fork
1 large skillet
1 spatula
pot holders

How to:

1. Spread peanut butter on 6 slices of bread.
2. Spread jelly on other 6 slices of bread.
3. Put 1 slice of each together to form sandwiches.
4. Break eggs into the mixing bowl. With fork, lightly beat eggs. Add milk, cinnamon, and salt, and mix together.
5. Melt butter or margarine in large skillet over medium heat.
6. Dip sandwiches in egg mixture, coating well.
7. Place in skillet and brown on both sides. Remove with spatula to plates and serve.

Serves 6.

SOLDIER'S SALAD ✡ (D)

Note: This recipe requires some preparation.

You will need:

1 lb. mild cheddar cheese, grated
2 hard-boiled eggs, grated
1 cup pecans, finely chopped
¾ cup mayonnaise
¼ cup sour cream
salt and pepper to taste
lettuce leaves
parsley for decoration

measuring cups
1 large mixing bowl
2 mixing spoons
1 small mixing bowl

How to:

1. In the large mixing bowl, mix together the cheese, eggs, and nuts.
2. In the small mixing bowl, mix together the mayonnaise and sour cream, and add to the cheese mixture.
3. Add salt and pepper and mix well.
4. Put mixture in the refrigerator until ready to serve.
5. Before serving, place lettuce leaves on each salad plate.
6. Put the salad mixture on the lettuce leaves and decorate with parsley.

Serves 8.

CONFEDERATE CHOCOLATE SHAKE ✡ ✡ (D)

You will need:

¾ cup milk
3 tbsp. chocolate syrup
1 pint vanilla ice cream

1 measuring cup
measuring spoons
1 blender
1 ice cream scoop or large spoon
2 straws, if you like

How to:

1. Pour milk into blender container. Add the chocolate syrup.
2. With adult help, cover and blend until smooth.
3. Add half the ice cream. Cover, blend until smooth.
4. Add the rest of the ice cream. Cover and blend until smooth.
5. Pour into glasses. Add the straw, if you like.

Serves 2.

LITTLE ROCK

The twins had so much fun in Vicksburg, they couldn't wait for the *Simcha Ship's* next stop. As soon as they awoke they asked their grandmother what was next. Grandmother took out the ship's schedule. She told the twins they were about to visit Little Rock, the capital of Arkansas.

Hannah and Hershel had never been to Arkansas. So when the ship's bell rang and the gangplank lowered, they were the first ones off the ship.

The twins really enjoyed Little Rock. They learned about the Quapaw Indians, who lived in central Arkansas before the white settlers came. But more exciting was the news that Little Rock had a zoo and a Wild River Country water park.

When Hannah and Hershel reached the zoo they were met by a guide. The guide said, "Hi, kids. Welcome to Little Rock Zoo. Here's where you'll see over 600 animals!"

"Wow!" said Hershel as they started to explore the zoo. Hershel grabbed Hannah's sleeve. "Look, Hannah, look over there."

"That's the zoo's great cat display," explained the guide, as he pointed to the jaguars, the snow leopard, the tigers, and the ferocious-looking lions.

"I've never seen so many wild animals together at one time," said Hannah, "not even in the circus."

As they rounded the bend, Hershel became even more excited. "Look, Grandma, look, there's the monkeys over there!"

"That's our great ape display, everyone's favorite," said the guide.

After a long tour on a hot day, the twins were looking forward to cooling off at Wild River Country, a water park.

In the bathhouse, Hershel and Hannah changed into their swimsuits and the fun began.

Off they ran toward the water attractions. First they went on "Thunder Alley" where they sat in little boats that took them high above the treetops on a ride of surprising twists and turns.

The ride went really fast. It was like being on the roller coaster, only in water. Hershel held on real tight and Hannah screamed the whole time.

Afterwards, Hannah told Hershel, "I got too frightened on

'Thunder Alley.' I want to play on the beach and build sand castles. I'm staying here. You can ride the 'Wild Surf' on the Arkansas Ocean by yourself."

Then Grandmother called to the children. "You two have had enough excitement for one day. It's time to dry off, change your clothes, and head back to the ship. We have to get back in time for Chef Lazér's next cooking class. You do want a taste of Arkansas, don't you?"

QUAPAW PIZZA ✡ ✡ (D)

Note: This recipe requires some preparation.

You will need:

1 bagel
1 tbsp. butter or margarine, melted
2 tbsp. tomato sauce
2 tbsp. shredded mozzarella cheese
2 sliced mushrooms or 2 sliced black olives, or both, if you like

measuring spoons
1 sharp knife
1 cutting board
1 cookie sheet or toaster oven tray
1 pastry brush
heavy oven mitts

How to:

1. Preheat the oven or toaster oven to 350°.
2. Slice bagel in half. Place bagel on cookie sheet or toaster tray, cut side up. Brush bagel with butter or margarine.
3. Spoon 1 tbsp. tomato sauce on each bagel slice and top with cheese, mushrooms, and sliced olives.
4. Bake for 5 minutes, or until the cheese begins to bubble.

Serves 1 to 2.

THUNDER ALLEY TOMATOES ✡ ✡ (D)

Note: This recipe requires some preparation.

You will need:

2 medium firm tomatoes
4 tbsp. canned green peas, drained
4 tbsp. grated cheddar cheese
¼ cup seasoned bread crumbs
1 tbsp. melted butter or margarine

1 measuring cup
measuring spoons
1 cutting board
1 paring knife
1 spoon
1 small mixing bowl
1 mixing spoon
1 small baking dish
heavy oven mitts

How to:

1. Preheat the oven to 375°.
2. Cut a ¼-inch slice from top of each tomato.
3. With a spoon, scoop out the inside of the tomato, being careful not to cut into the bottom.
4. Lightly fill tomatoes with drained green peas and set aside.
5. Mix the cheese, bread crumbs, and melted butter or margarine together.
6. Place the tomatoes in the baking dish. Sprinkle cheese mixture on top of each tomato.
7. Put tomatoes in oven and bake for 15 minutes.

Serves 2.

LITTLE "ROCKS" ✡ ✡ (D)

You will need:

6-oz. package semi-sweet chocolate chips
½ cup graham cracker crumbs
1 cup pecan pieces

measuring cups
1 double boiler
1 wooden spoon
1 teaspoon
wax paper
pot holders

How to:

1. Fill the bottom of the double boiler with about 1 inch of water.
2. Put the chocolate chips in the top of the double boiler. Over a medium flame, heat the chocolate until melted.
3. Stir in the graham cracker crumbs and the pecan pieces.
4. Drop the mixture from a teaspoon onto the waxed paper.
5. Let stand until cool, then remove from wax paper.

Makes about 15 "rocks."

MEMPHIS

Grandmother checked the bulletin board for the ship's next stop. It was going to be a day in Memphis.

"Memphis, 'the city on the bluffs,'" Hannah and Hershel heard the captain tell some of the passengers. The twins remembered what bluffs were. They were the hills in Vicksburg where battles were fought.

Hershel said, "I can't wait to visit Memphis. Maybe I'll hear some war stories about battles on the bluff."

However, the twins were in for quite a surprise and more fun than they had ever had!

They started the day eating breakfast at the hotel that is home to the "Peabody ducks." Just as they finished eating, at exactly 11:00 o'clock, the world-famous "Peabody ducks" strutted through the lobby to the music of the "King Cotton March." Everyone clapped while the ducks marched in time to the music and got into a fountain in the middle of the lobby. The twins were sorry they couldn't get back at 5:00 o'clock, when the ducks march back to their roof-top house. But Grandmother had a lot she wanted to see and show them.

Grandmother said, "You've seen everything you wanted, now it's my turn." So off the group went to Graceland. On the way there, Grandmother told the twins all about Graceland, the home of Elvis Presley, who she said was the "King of Rock and Roll." Hannah and Hershel laughed together when Grandmother told them how when she was a teenager she would scream and jump up and down every time he sang.

When they got to Graceland, they couldn't believe how many gold records Elvis had made!

After Graceland, they went to the Pink Palace. At first they thought they were going to a king's castle, but it was even better than that. It turned out to be a museum and planetarium with dinosaur fossils and a roaring, stomping Triceratops dinosaur that looked so real it even scared Grandmother. Then a movie at the planetarium took them through space and time.

Before the twins knew it, it was time to go back to the *Simcha Ship*, where Chef Lazér was waiting to teach them Memphis cooking.

MEMPHIS MEATBURGERS ✡ ✡ (M)

Note: This recipe requires some preparation.

You will need:

1 lb. ground meat
¼ cup bread crumbs
1 egg, lightly beaten
1 tsp. salt
½ tsp. pepper
¼ cup ketchup

measuring cups
measuring spoons
1 mixing bowl
1 mixing spoon
1 9-inch baking pan
heavy oven mitts

How to:

1. Preheat the oven to 450°.
2. Mix the ground meat with the bread crumbs, egg, salt, pepper, and ketchup.
3. Shape the mixture into patties about 1 inch thick. Put patties in baking pan.
4. Bake for 10 to 12 minutes.

Makes 6 meat patties.

BAKED POTATOES ON THE BLUFF ✡ ✡ (P)

You will need:

2 baking potatoes
2 tbsp. pareve margarine

1 tablespoon
towel or paper towels
1 oven rack
heavy oven mitts
1 paring knife

How to:

1. Preheat the oven to 400°.
2. Wash the potatoes well and pat dry.
3. Put on rack in oven and bake for 1 hour.
4. Put on oven mitts and carefully remove the potatoes.
5. With paring knife, make a 2-inch slit on top of potatoes and place 1 tbsp. pareve margarine in the slit of each potato before serving.

Serves 2.

PINK PALACE APPLE SAUCE ✡ ✡ (P)

You will need:

4 medium apples
¼ cup strawberry soda pop
¼ cup sugar
¼ tsp. cinnamon

measuring cups
measuring spoons
1 vegetable peeler
1 apple corer
1 paring knife
1 cutting board
1 2-qt. pot with cover
1 mixing spoon
1 deep bowl
pot holders

How to:

1. Peel and core apples, then cut apples into 1-inch pieces.
2. In the pot put the apple pieces, soda pop, sugar, and cinnamon. Mix together with the spoon.
3. Put the cover on the pot and cook over medium heat until the apples are soft (about 30 minutes).
4. Pour apples into deep bowl and serve either warm or cold.

Serves 4.

GRACELAND GREEN BEAN CASEROLE ✡ ✡ (P)

You will need:

2 16-oz. cans green beans
1 10½-oz. can pareve condensed mushroom soup
1 tsp. lemon juice
½ of a 3-oz. can French-fried onions

measuring spoons
1 can opener
1 colander
1½-qt. casserole dish
1 rubber scraper
heavy oven mitts

How to:

1. Preheat the oven to 350°.
2. Drain the beans in the colander and put them into the casserole dish.
3. With the rubber scraper, scrape the mushroom soup out of the can onto the beans.
4. Add the lemon juice and stir with the scraper until well mixed.
5. Put the casserole in the oven.
6. Bake for 30 minutes, then, using the oven mitts, remove the casserole from the oven.
7. Sprinkle the French-fried onions over the top of the casserole and put the casserole back into oven.
8. Bake for 5 more minutes, until onions are hot and brown.

Serves 6.

HANNIBAL

Hershel and Hannah had just finished telling the class that their last stop was Hannibal, Missouri, when Ms. Farrell interrupted. "I want to remind you that Hannibal, Missouri, was where Mark Twain grew up," she said. "If you remember, he wrote the stories about Tom Sawyer, Becky Thatcher, Aunt Polly, and Huckleberry Finn."

"Grandmother thought the best way for us to see Hannibal and learn about Mark Twain was to take the Twainland Choo Choo Express," Hershel began. "And as usual, Grandmother was right. Everything we saw on the ride had to do with Mark Twain's life and his stories."

"We saw statues of Tom and Huck and one of Mark Twain himself," Hannah chimed in. "And we rode by the Lighthouse. Grandmother reminded us that the Lighthouse was built on Cardiff Hill and this was where Tom and Huck visited with Widow Douglas and ate her homemade ice cream."

The twins had been busy looking from one side of the train to another when they heard the clang of the train bell. That meant the train was making its first stop, which was Mark Twain's boyhood home—the same home that became the home of Aunt Polly in his stories.

The twins were excited to think that they would be visiting Aunt Polly's house, where Tom and Sid and Mary spent so much of their time.

Grandmother turned to them and said, "See the white picket fence on the side? Remember when Tom tricked his friends into helping him paint? Well, this is the fence."

"Oh, I remember that part of the story," said Hannah.

As the twins headed back to the train they became even more excited, for they knew the next stop was the Mark Twain Cave, and they had never been to a cave before.

The train came to a screeching halt near the entrance to the Mark Twain Cave. The tour guide was there waiting for them. Hershel and Hannah couldn't wait to explore the same cave Tom Sawyer and Becky Thatcher did many years ago.

It was cold and damp and spooky, even though there were lights. Hannah said to Hershel, "Imagine how scary it must have been for Tom and Becky when there were no lights!"

But Hershel said, "I like it! It's a real adventure, just like Tom

Sawyer said it was. And it's a great way to end our trip."

Walking back from the cave and getting back on the train, the twins looked a little sad, for they knew that this was indeed the end of their trip and that their vacation was almost over. But knowing that Chef Lazér was waiting for them back on the *Simcha Ship* for one more cooking class made them feel happy again.

HANNIBAL HOT DOGS ✡ ✡ (M)

You will need:

1 cup water
4 hot dogs
4 hot dog buns, split
ketchup and mustard, if
   you like

1 measuring cup
1 2-qt. pot with cover
1 pair tongs
1 table knife
pot holders

How to:

1. Pour water into the 2-qt. pot. Put pot on stove to cook over high heat.
2. When water comes to a boil, put the hot dogs into the boiling water, one at a time.
3. When the water begins to boil again, put the cover on the pot and turn off the burner.
4. Let the hot dogs stay in the covered pot for 8 to 10 minutes.
5. Use the table knife to spread ketchup or mustard on the hot dog buns, if you like.
6. Remove lid from the pot. Use the tongs to lift out each hot dog and put on a bun.

Serves 4.

BECKY'S BAKED BEANS ✡ ✡ (P)

You will need:

3 tbsp. vegetable oil
1 onion
2 16-oz. cans vegetarian baked beans
2 tbsp. brown sugar
2 tbsp. ketchup
1 tbsp. Worcestershire sauce
1 tbsp. prepared mustard

measuring spoons
10-inch skillet
1 paring knife
1 cutting board
1 wooden spoon
1 can opener
1½-qt. casserole dish
1 slotted spoon
heavy oven mitts

How to:

1. Preheat the oven to 350°.
2. Pour the oil into the skillet.
3. Peel and chop the onion. Add the chopped onion to the oil in the skillet. Turn the burner to medium-low heat.
4. Cook the onion until it is soft, but not brown. Stir once in a while with the wooden spoon.
5. When the onions are cooked, turn off the burner.
6. Pour the beans into the casserole dish. Stir in the brown sugar, ketchup, Worcestershire, and mustard and mix well.
7. With the slotted spoon, take the onions from the skillet and stir into the bean mixture.
8. Put the casserole into the oven. Bake for 1 hour.
9. Use heavy oven mitts to remove casserole from oven.

Serves 6.

MARK TWAIN'S CAVE COOKIES ✡ ✡ (P)

You will need:

1 18.5-oz. box of cake mix, either yellow or devil food
2 eggs
½ cup vegetable oil
raisins, nuts, chocolate chips, if you like

1 measuring cup
1 large mixing bowl
1 large mixing spoon
1 teaspoon
1 cookie sheet
heavy oven mitts
1 spatula

How to:

1. Preheat the oven to 350°.
2. Put the cake mix, eggs, and vegetable oil in the mixing bowl.
3. With a mixing spoon, mix well.
4. If you like, add either nuts, raisins, or chocolate chips, and mix into the batter.
5. With the teaspoon, drop spoonfuls of batter on the ungreased cookie sheet, about 2 inches apart.
6. Put cookie sheet in oven and bake for 8 to 10 minutes.
7. With heavy oven mitts, remove the cookie sheet. The cookies will get harder as they cool. When the cookies cool, remove from the cookie sheet with a spatula.

Makes about 8 dozen cookies.

SHALOM

After the last cooking class, Hershel and Hannah hugged Chef Lazér and thanked him for making their trip up the Mississippi River so special. Then they said good-bye to all their shipmates and promised to write each other when they got home.

When the twins returned to their cabin, Grandmother was busy with the last-minute packing. The twins looked around to make sure they weren't leaving anything behind. They couldn't believe their trip was coming to an end. They had loved every minute of it and realized how lucky they were to have a grandmother like theirs. They grabbed Grandmother and hugged her.

"We love you. We're so glad you're our grandmother."

Grandmother held the twins tightly, and said softly to them, "I love you both, too. You are both very special to me."

As the *Simcha Ship* lowered its gangplank, Hershel and Hannah were standing by the rail, looking at the crowd of people below and trying to find their parents.

"There they are," cried Hershel.

"There's Mother and Daddy. I see them," an excited Hannah added.

The captain of the *Simcha Ship* and Chef Lazér were standing on deck, side by side, greeting the passengers as they were ready to leave. The captain saluted the twins and gave each of them a captain's cap as a souvenir so they would always remember their cruise. Then Chef Lazér also gave the twins a souvenir. It was a cookbook with all the recipes they made in their cooking classes.

The twins thanked the captain and Chef Lazér. Then, putting the caps on their heads and holding onto their books, they ran down the ramp. They turned and waved good-bye to the captain and crew of the *Simcha Ship*.

Mother and Daddy greeted Hershel and Hannah with open arms and kisses, and the twins were already chatting away with news of their trip. Poor Grandmother! She barely got a word in. But she knew it was, indeed, a wonderful trip, one where the twins learned all about history and geography—and even cooking.

We'd say that Hershel and Hannah were lucky to have such a wonderful trip with their Grandmother. Wouldn't you?

INDEX

DESSERTS
   Ben-Yeahs 20, 21
   Little "Rocks" 44
   Mark Twain's Cave Cookies . 56
   Natchez Nosh 32
   Pink Palace Apple Sauce . . . 49

DRINKS
   Confederate
      Chocolate Shake 37
   Quarter Quencher 32

FOWL
   Capitol Chicken 26

MEAT
   Hannibal Hot Dogs 54
   Memphis Meatburgers 47

PASTA
   Spaghetti
      with Swamp Sauce 27

PIZZA
   Quapaw Pizza 42

SALAD
   Nutti Fruit Salad 28
   Plantation Potato Salad 31
   Soldier's Salad 36

SANDWICHES
   Hershel's
      "Hero" Sandwich 32
   Peanutty Toast 35

SEAFOOD
   Hershel's
      "Hero" Sandwich 32
   Paddlewheel Fish Balls 19

VEGETABLES
   Baked Potatoes
      on the Bluff 48
   Becky's Baked Beans 55
   Cornsicles 20
   Graceland Green Bean
      Casserole 50
   Thunder Alley Tomatoes . . . 43

Made in the USA
Monee, IL
28 April 2026

49137081R00038